The **Essential** B

BMW B

TWINS

All air-cooled R45, R50, R60, R65, R75, R80, R90,
R100, RS, RT & LS (not GS) models 1969 to 1994

Your marque expert:
Peter Henshaw

VELOCE PUBLISHING
THE PUBLISHER OF FINE AUTOMOTIVE BOOKS

www.veloce.co.uk

First published in April 2017 by Veloce Publishing Limited, Veloce House, Parkway Farm Business Park, Middle Farm Way, Poundbury, Dorchester, Dorset, DT1 3AR, England.
Fax 01305 250479/e-mail info@veloce.co.uk/web www.veloce.co.uk or www.velocebooks.com.

ISBN: 978-1-78711-005-2 UPC: 6-36847-01005-8

Readers with ideas for automotive books, or books on other transport or related hobby subjects, are invited to write to the editorial director of Veloce Publishing at the above address.
British Library Cataloguing in Publication Data – A catalogue record for this book is available from the British Library.
Typesetting, design and page make-up all by Veloce Publishing Ltd on Apple Mac. Printed in India by Imprint Digital Ltd.

Introduction
– the purpose of this book

BMW flat-twins (boxers) built up to 1994 – 'airheads,' to use their colloquial name – have long split motorcycling fraternity down the middle. Like Harley-Davidson V-twins, they have devoted owners who would buy nothing else, and equally vehement detractors, who maintain that they are too slow, boring, and oddball to be taken seriously.

Airheads are certainly different to other motorcycles: for years they were the only flat-twin on the market (apart from the Russian-made Ural, which, in any case, has BMW roots). They were part of a design philosophy that saw a motorcycle as a functional tool, able to cover long distances at high speeds with complete reliability; hence features such as shaft drive and a dry single-plate clutch, and an almost legendary toughness that makes 100,000 miles easily achievable, with several bikes having covered well over 200,000 miles.

Of course, there is a downside to this unique character. Airheads are notorious for several things, including a slow and clunky gearchange, a lack of top end power, and the strange effects on handling of torque reaction. Some of these side effects were always exaggerated, while others were mitigated or even remedied over the years. Not that sales suffered – if you include the legendary GS adventure tourer (covered by a different book in this series), about 500,000 airhead BMWs have been built, and many of these are still on the road: a testament to their ultimate reliability. With so many still active, spares supply is excellent, with anything not available new usually offered secondhand. There is also a very strong club following for airheads, with generations of knowledgeable riders able to help newcomers.

Above all, these are practical bikes. Simple machines that are designed to be used. Shaft drive cuts down on maintenance requirements, the big fuel tank gives a long range, and most of them (especially the faired RT) are supremely comfortable, even over very long distances. It's hardly surprising that they became the bikes of choice, not just for police forces all over the world, but for global travellers as well.

This book is a straightforward guide to buying an airhead secondhand. It doesn't list all the minutiae of model changes, or colours for each year, but hopefully it will help you avoid buying a dud. It covers all BMW airheads (apart from the GS and ST) from 1969 to the end of production in 1994. The 1969 /5 bikes were a real departure for BMW, making a less expensive machine that sought to compete with the Japanese and European rivals, though they still weren't cheap. The big airheads died in the mid-1980s, but returned by popular demand, and enjoyed a last burst of popularity before production finally ended.

Today, they make a really good choice as a practical classic bike that can be used day to day, even for commuting. BMW airheads were designed to be working bikes, and still function as such.

Thanks go to all those who made this book possible: Graham Walkley and Aaron Wellington, Roger Fogg, staff and volunteers at the VMCC library, and finally Sam Manicom, Birgit Schunemann and Mark Manley, who have ridden their airheads all over the world.

Mick McMillan rode round the world on this R65, met his wife, came home, and had a family!

BMW airheads are plentiful, affordable, and make good practical classics.

Contents

The Essential Buyer's Guide™ currency
At the time of publication a BG unit of currency "●" equals approximately
£1.00/US$1.27/Euro 1.19. Please adjust to suit current exchange rates.

1 Is it the right bike for you?
– marriage guidance

Tall and short riders
BMW airheads are physically big, fairly heavy, and have a highish seat, which shorter riders might find intimidating. The R45 and pre-1984 R65 are smaller.

Running costs
Fairly modest by big bike standards. The R90/100 give 40-45mpg, the R80 and 65 a more frugal 50-55mpg if ridden gently. And there's no chain/sprockets to replace.

Maintenance
Easy and undemanding. Again, no chain and sprockets to think about, and all the regular items – oil, filters and tappet adjustment – are straightforward to do. Some more complex jobs will need a specialist.

Useability
Very good, compared to some contemporaries. BMWs were always practical bikes, and the airheads are no exception – you could commute to work on one of these.

Parts availability
Excellent. With 500,000 airheads built over 30 years, there is a huge market for spares, and most parts are available new or secondhand.

Unleaded fuel
All twin-shock airheads were designed to run on leaded fuel, though many will have since had valve seats replaced. Most monoshock bikes (1985-on) could cope with unleaded from new.

Parts costs
Expensive, if you go for genuine BMW parts, which are readily available, but cheaper pattern parts are available, too, from the specialists.

Insurance group
Of the 17 insurance groups in the UK, the R80 is in group 8 and R100 in group 9, so they shouldn't be expensive to insure, especially on a limited mileage classic policy.

Investment potential
Solid, but not blue chip. The R90S has always been the stand-out investment, but all the others are increasing in value slowly. The original RT and RS are worth saving now.

Foibles
The airhead's almost unique mechanical layout has endeared it to thousands, but it takes some getting used to.

Plus points
All round day to day useability, reliability, plus surprisingly good performance and handling.

Minus points
Weight, slow gearchange, and the image of an 'old man's bike' still lingers.

Alternatives
Most obvious is the Moto Guzzi V-twin, with a similar idiosyncratic character, large twin-cylinder engine and shaft drive. The Russian-made Ural has a lot in common with airheads, but usually comes with a sidecar attached (which can be good or bad, depending on your point of view).

A well-used and well-loved R75/7 – they suit some people very well indeed.

The badge doesn't lie – these are quality motorcycles.

2 Cost considerations
– affordable, or a money pit?

BMW parts have a reputation for being expensive, and by and large that's accurate. However, they are good quality, and many genuine parts are still available for older bikes.

Cheaper pattern parts are also available for many items – if sold by a BMW specialist, these should be a safe bet.

Although some parts, such as complete fairings or crankcases, aren't available new, there are lots of secondhand options around.

Prices listed below are from a BMW specialist, and all parts are genuine BMW unless otherwise stated.

Complete restoration (basket case to concours) – around ●x10,000

Alternator rotor (pattern) – ●x60
Brake pads – ●x35
Battery – ●x75
Carburettor overhaul kit (pattern) – ●x23
Clutch cable – ●x23
Clutch plate – ●x67
Driveshaft – ●x258
Exhaust downpipes (pr, stainless) – ●x209
Fairing panel (RT l/h upper) – ●x55
Fork oil seals (pr) – ●x15
Fork stanchions (ea, pattern) – ●x149
Gasket set (whole engine) – ●x53
Headlight reflector – ●x142
Switch cluster (left-hand) – ●x91
Piston (ea) – ●x114
Pushrod (ea) – ●x32
Rear shocks (Hagon, pr) – ●x210
Screen (RT) – ●x226
Seat – ●x144
Service kit (filters, plugs, gaskets) – ●x40
Silencers (stainless, pr) – ●x338
Timing chain kit – ●x72
Valves (ea, pattern) – ●x13
Wheel bearing (ea) – ●x13
Wiring loom – ●x189

The flat-twins are well catered for with spare parts – most things are obtainable.

Binnacles are available; the instruments are trickier to find.

3 Living with a BMW Boxer
– will you get along together?

BMW flat-twins don't suit everyone, but it's their almost unique mechanical layout – Ural apart, this was the only flat-twin available for decades – that makes many riders refuse to even try one. That, and the lingering suspicion that these are boring bikes for earnest middle-aged men who sport beards, and have a very serious attitude to motorcycling.

It's true that the flat-twin is not a snappy revver, that the gearchange is slow, and that the bikes are heavy (though little more than contemporary 750s and 900s). However, they are also faster than you might think, handle surprisingly well, and are very enjoyable to ride. Not only that, but BMW airheads are probably the most all-round useable classic bikes of their era – they have high speed stamina and need less intensive maintenance.

But let's get the downsides out of the way first, because these can be enough to put off some potential owners altogether. The R80, 90 and 100 are physically big bikes with seat heights of about 820mm, and shorter riders might be more comfortable on the R45 or 65, especially the early machines with a lower seat.

Early bikes, even the /5 and /6, are perfectly useable day to day.

Over 98,000 miles showing on this R100 – six-figure mileages aren't uncommon.

The engine speed clutch gives all airheads a ponderous gearchange, which can be clunky and 'clashy' at low speeds – it was improved from 1983, but it's still not exactly slick, and has been likened to driving a car with a non-syncromesh gearbox. The front drum brake on the /5, especially the faster R75/5, is not up to modern stopping standards, and the mechanical layout brought foibles of its own – blip the throttle at a standstill, and the bike will twist to one side; move off, and the rear rises. BMW fans will say that you just get used to the foibles, but they are worth bearing in mind.

Fortunately, there are also plenty of upsides to airhead ownership. These bikes are relatively simple, certainly compared to contemporary Japanese or Italian machines, and well built. They are strong, easy to work on, and can cover high mileages very reliably – it's no coincidence that BMWs are a favourite for touring, nor that they have been used by police forces all over the world. The shaft drive is one of the key features, offered at a time when chain drive was universal amongst motorcycles. Although heavier than a chain, it cuts out a lot of maintenance chores, and if you are looking at doing greater mileage, is a real bonus. The big fuel tank, a generous 24 litres on most bikes, is another aid to long distance riding. Running costs are relatively modest, with a typical tyre life of 7000 miles rear, 10,000 front, and fuel consumption about the same as contemporaries.

BMWs are long-lived by bike standards. On most motorcycles of the 1970s and '80s, a mileage of 50,000 is unusually high, but a 50,000-mile airhead is nicely run in, and given regular maintenance, they can happily run to 100,000 miles or more without major bottom end work. Of course, the downside is that an airhead showing 50,000 miles may have already been 'around the clock' once or even twice. Fortunately, this mechanical reliability is backed up by good Bosch electrics, with a powerful 280W alternator fitted from the /6 models onwards.

Big-fairing RT makes a superb tourer.

BMW boxers have suffered (certainly in the popular conception) from an apparent lack of power compared to contemporary bikes, and on paper that's certainly true – with 57bhp, the R75/5 had less power than any Japanese 750. In practice, good low- and mid-range torque, especially on the bigger bikes, gives them good performance in the real world. All (with the possible exception of the R45) are capable of cruising at 70-80mph all day, two-up with luggage, although the R100 will be more relaxed at this speed than will an R65. Autobahns permitting, the R100RS and RT are capable of far higher cruising speeds, the rider cocooned behind that superb fairing.

Handling, too, is a lot better than the folk image would suggest. Airheads are not light, 'flickable' bikes, but they have a strong rigid frame, supple suspension and (early front drum apart) good brakes into the bargain. They do reward smooth riding – heavy braking produces a lot of fork dive, but, given that, they can be pushed along twisty roads very rapidly, and rest assured that the horizontally-opposed cylinders do not seriously limit cornering clearance.

The flat-twin engine also has near perfect balance, giving very smooth running for a twin. The lack of vibration, the soft, long-travel suspension and good seat make these very comfy bikes that can rack up 400-500-mile days without a problem for rider and pillion. Passengers are of course well catered for, with a wide and long seat which again is good over distance – the exception is the early R100RS, whose upswept seat is more one-and-a-half-up, rather than two-up.

Perhaps one of the airhead's biggest advantages as a classic choice is that the basic layout is available across a wide range of bikes. Leaving aside the successful GS line-up (dealt with by a separate book in this series) this spans everything from the mild-mannered 35bhp R45 to the sporty and glamorous R90S and R100RS, topped out by the ultimate tourers of R80RT and R100RT.

This still doesn't mean that there's a BMW airhead to suit everyone, but all of them are easy to live with and capable of covering big miles with little hassle.

4 Relative values
– which model for you?

Range availability
R50, 60, 75 & 80 up to 1984
1969-73 R50/5
1969-73 R60/5
1969-73 R75/5
1973-76 R60/6
1973-76 R75/6
1976-82 R60/7
1976-79 R75/7
1977-84 R80/7
1982-84 R80RT

R90 & 100 up to 1984
1973-76 R90/6
1973-76 R90S
1976-84 R100RS
1976-80 R100/7
1976-80 R100S
1978-84 R100RT
1980-84 R100CS

R45 & 65 up to 1985
1978-85 R45
1978-85 R65
1981-85 R65LS

R65, 80 & 100 Mono 1984 on
1984-95 R80
1984-95 R80RT
1985-93 R65
1986-92 R100RS
1987-95 R100RT
1991-94 R80R
1991-95 R100R
1993-95 R100R Mystic

All stated percentage values are in relation to the /5 models current prices for which can be found in various classic bike value guides.

R50, 60, 75 & 80 up to 1984
This range of airheads – the /5, /6 and /7, covering 1969-84, is the most 'classic' of the whole lot, with a front drum brake on the /5 (and R60/6), plus twin rear shocks and contact breaker ignition right up to 1981.
Launched in late 1969 as the first of the new generation BMWs, the /5 range consisted of the R50/5, R60/5 and R75/5. They were highly successful, and

the R75 was most popular, with over 38,000 sold, followed by the R60 (nearly 23,000), while the R50 (less than 8000 made) is now quite rare. The R50 had quite limited performance, but the R60 was usefully quicker, able to cruise at 80mph, and the R75 faster still, to the extent that its front drum brake is marginal for the performance. /5 bikes are instantly recognisable by their combined speedometer and rev counter – all other bikes had separate instruments in a binnacle.

Early /5s suffered from a high-speed weave, which could be disconcerting, and was only rectified when BMW extended the wheelbase by 50mm, by adding an extra section into the swingarm – this change was made in 1972, and the extra welded-in section is just visible near the front of the swingarm. There were few changes to the /5 in its lifetime, though in 1972 BMW did attempt to jazz up its appearance with a smaller 18-litre tank in place of the standard 24-litre, with added chrome, plus more chrome on the side panels. This lasted only a year, and is rare, especially in Europe.

The /6, launched in 1973, saw the R50 dropped and an R90 added (see next section), while the R60 became increasingly confined to fleet users such as police forces. All /6s incorporated a whole string of major improvements, as BMW sought to keep the airheads abreast of Japanese and European rivals. The most obvious changes were a front disc brake on the R75, a five-speed gearbox (though the change wasn't improved), and a separate speedo and rev counter. The styling was brought up to date a little, with a less bulbous (but still 22-litre) fuel tank, and a conventional ignition key in place of the traditional BMW plunger, for which any key would fit any bike. Drilled brake discs were fitted from 1975.

The /7 from 1976 saw few major changes, the most obvious being the squared-off rocker covers and new cylinder barrel finning to give a more modern appearance, while the R60 adopted the front disc brake. There were some minor changes to the valve gear, including the use of alloy tappets.

Perhaps more significant was the replacement in 1978 of the R75/7 with the R80/7, thought by many to be the best all-round compromise between performance, running costs and value. This bike became a stalwart of the range, with several changes over the years, which applied to the whole range: single-row camchain from 1979, while 1981 saw several changes including a lighter flywheel, Nikasil coated bores, electronic ignition plus Brembo disc brakes replacing the previous ATEs.

An R80RT combined all the R100RT features, with the smaller 798cc engine in 1982, and actually outsold its big brother by three to one, while in '84 both this and the R80/7 were given the Monolever (single shock) rear end, new front forks and similar alloy wheels to the K series.

Strengths/weaknesses: Airheads with the most classic appeal, but still useable day to day. Front drum brake, and lacks the high speed cruising abilities of later, bigger airheads.

/5: 100%
/7: 62%
R80RT: 46%

R90 & 100 up to 1984

If one airhead stands out, it's the R90S – for all the attention it receives, you might think that this most glamorous BMW of its time was also the best seller, but in fact it only lasted three years and was outsold by the far more ordinary looking R90/6!

The R90S was BMW's recognition that the R75 was being rapidly overtaken by a new generation of 750 and 900cc superbikes. And it wasn't just performance – the new flagship required added pizzazz as well. The R90S was certainly fast, the familiar flat-twin bored out to 898cc, with a higher 9.5:1 compression ratio and 38mm Dell Orto carburettors resulting in 67bhp at 7500rpm and a top speed of 125mph. Twin front discs, gaiterless forks, and a headlight fairing were other instant recognition factors, as was the standard colour scheme of Smoke Grey. Later joined by Smoke Orange, this was applied by hand, so it could be said that no two bikes were identical. The R90S, which certainly did the job of raising BMW's profile, also featured a small tail fairing, a steering damper and lower bars, while the headlight fairing housed a voltmeter and clock.

RT fairing gives very comfortable high speed cruising.

Of course, all this had to be paid for, and the R90S was the most expensive production bike of its time, twice the price of a contemporary Norton Commando or Honda CB750. But it did sell, and its profile was boosted by race wins, something not seen from BMW for many years – Reg Pridmore won the US Production Championship in 1976 on an R90S, and there were victories at the Isle of Man TT and Daytona.

If you find an original R100RS, they're worth saving.

With a track record like this, the R90S is now the most sought-after airhead, though it has to be said that the standard R90/6 is only slightly slower. With Bing carburettors in place of the Dell Ortos, this offered just 60bhp from the 898cc flat-twin, though with no fairings or fancy paint job, it could be mistaken for a R75/6, or even an R60. Given that the S is such an icon, unscrupulous sellers could be tempted to dress up an R90/6 as its racier brother. However, there are plenty of recognition points for a genuine S, with black barrels and a flush filler cap being among the other differences.

R90S is the most sought-after of all BMW airheads.

But nothing stands still, and in September 1976 the R90S were replaced by the naked R100/7 and dramatically faired R100RS. The latter made a huge impact, the first production motorcycle to have a full fairing as standard. The bodywork had been painstakingly developed in a wind tunnel, and it paid off, cocooning the rider in a pocket of still air at 100mph but without looking like the proverbial barn door. Underneath it all, this was really an updated R90, the flat-twin bored out to 980cc, offering 70bhp in the RS, or 60bhp in the R100/7, which had smaller 32mm carburettors and a lower compression ratio.

The RS works best at high speed cruising – at lower speeds its narrow and lowish bars put quite a bit weight on the wrists, but as a milestone design it is one of the greats. One collectable variant is the rare Motorsport version in white with red and blue highlights, as just 200 of these were made. RS prices are currently rising, and their investment potential looks good.

The RS was joined in 1978 by the RT, the ultimate touring airhead, also with an aerodynamic fairing, but with higher, wider bars for an all-day comfortable riding position. Like the RS, it gave superb weather protection, but was equally comfortable at lower speeds, and even featured fresh air vents for hot days. Krauser panniers were standard, and most RTs around today will have some sort of luggage system. Boge Nivomat self-levelling shocks were fitted from new, but 30 years later, on many bikes these will have been replaced with standard shocks. Both RS and RT airheads in standard form are worth seeking out, as many have been stripped of their fairings to fuel the custom boom in cafe racers or street scramblers – as new fairings aren't available, this is certain to create a shortage of original bikes in the future.

The R100 family was soon joined by the R100S (with R90S style headlight fairing), which was renamed R100CS in 1980, while the R100/7 became R100T. In 1981, all R100s had the same raft of changes as the smaller airheads: lighter flywheel, Nikasil bores, electronic ignition and Brembo brakes. There were few changes to the R100 until 1984, when the range was dropped in favour of the new water-cooled K100s.

Strengths/weaknesses: Good performance in a practical package, R90S glamour, R100RS investment potential. Not as sweet as R65/80.

R90/6: 105%
R90S: 200%
R100s (except RS): 60%
R100RS: 86%

R45 & 65 up to 1985
The R45 and R65 were a determined attempt by BMW to return to the midrange market, and rather than fit a smaller engine to the R80, they did the job properly. The R45/R65 were smaller versions of the big airheads, with their own frame with a shorter wheelbase and (until 1980) lower seat height. So the 1978-80 baby BMWs can be the best choice for shorter riders.

R45 shouldn't be dismissed, and there are plenty around.

Otherwise, these are miniature airheads with exactly the same mechanical layout as all the others, with the exception of the smaller engines and a drum rear brake. The R45 used a 473cc flat-twin offering 35bhp, though for the German market there was an R45N with 27bhp, to fit into learner laws. The R65 had a more useful 45bhp, thanks to its larger capacity, bigger inlet vales and 38mm Bing carburettors, though it was still in a mild state of tune.

The R45 is derided by some as being too slow, but for gentle touring and leisure rides it's perfectly adequate. Its bigger brother is a lot more relaxed at higher speeds, able to cruise at 70-80mph, though it still isn't in the same long-striding league as an R80 or

Early R45/65s are smaller than the R80/100, with a lower seat.

100. It also has an annoying vibration patch at 55mph in top, a real drawback in the USA market when that was the speed limit.

Both bikes have good brakes and handling (the single front disc and rear drum is up to the performance), with the same concept of soft, long-travel suspension as the bigger airheads, and the R65 in particular is thought to be the most nimble airhead of all. Despite the smaller engines, they aren't much more economical than an R80/7 because they are only about 10kg lighter, and have lower gearing.

There were very few changes to the R45/65 until the end of production of the twin-shock bikes in 1985 – the 1985-on R65 Monolever is dealt with below, though the R65's power was boosted to 50bhp for 1981, when both bikes were given a longer wheelbase and electronic ignition. In the same year, the sportier R65LS joined the range, styled by Hans Muth (who also penned the Suzuki Katana) with a wedge-shaped nose fairing, lower bars, twin front discs and brighter colours – it wasn't a great success, seen as too brash by BMW standards. But, as fewer than 7000 were made, that should make it more collectable in the future.

Specific problems with the R45/65 are few, though the alloy wheels can crack, and valve heads have been known to detach on higher mileage 1978-79 bikes. The baby airheads were very popular, with around 28,000 R45s and over 29,000 R65s built up to 1985, so there are plenty still around. They are currently the cheapest route into airhead ownership.

Strengths/weaknesses: Slightly smaller, lighter and sweeter than the big airheads, and generally cheaper to buy. But also slower, and less relaxed at speed.

R45/65: 40%

R65, 80 & 100 1984 on

In the early 1980s, BMW's plan was to drop the airhead flat-twins, certainly the R100s, in favour of the new K-series family of water-cooled three- and four-cylinder bikes. But it didn't turn out like that, because the twins had such a strong following – although the GS was proving a huge success, there was still a healthy demand for roadster and touring airheads as well.

So the mid- to late-

Post-1984 bikes, including this R80, adopted the GS Monolever rear end.

1980s saw the complete range return – R65, R80 and R100 – all of them with the R80GS's Monolever rear suspension with the driveshaft acting as a single-sided swingarm, and a single rear shock. The R65 and R80 were launched in 1985, and were now very similar bikes, the 65 taking on the 80's frame and cycle parts. The R65's power output was tweaked again, this time to move the torque peak down from 6500rpm to a much more relaxed 3500rpm. Smoother than the R80, it was only slightly cheaper to buy and fewer were sold – 8260 until production ended.

The R80 and 80RT carried on in Monolever form, along with new forks and alloy

R80RT Monolever offered the same touring package as before.

Final R100 Mystic reverted to spoked wheels and rounded rocker boxes.

wheels similar to those of the K-series. The rockers were modified to reduce top end noise, otherwise this long-running and popular airhead continued to sell well – over 17,000 R80s and just over 22,000 80RTs were built before production ended in 1994.

Meanwhile, demand for a big airhead compelled BMW to relaunch the R100RS in 1986 and the RT a year later, both of them using the Monolever rear end, but now with a milder 60bhp version of the 980cc flat-twin, with lower compression ratio and smaller carburettors – BMW's high speed flagship was now the four-cylinder K-series.

In 1991, the R100s received the latest Paralever rear end, now with an extra strut parallel to the driveshaft, and a second UJ in the shaft itself, which finally banished torque reaction.

The final R100 variants underlined that the bike's heritage was one of its main attractions, and the 1991 R100R came with spoked wheels instead of alloys; even the old rounded rocker covers made a return. It was a great success, and over 20,000 were sold. The Mystic, a limited edition R100R with exra chrome and skimpier side panels, appeared in 1993. Production of all R100s finally ended in October 1994, though some airheads were undoubtedly registered the following year.

Strengths/weaknesses: As previous, but with improved gearchange and rear end.

See previous value.

5 Before you view
– be well informed

To avoid a wasted journey, and the disappointment of finding that the bike does not match your expectations, it will help if you're very clear about what questions you want to ask before you pick up the phone. Some of these points might appear basic, but when you're excited about the prospect of buying your dream bike, it's amazing how some of the most obvious things slip the mind ... Also check the current values of the model you are interested in online, and in classic bike magazine classified ads.

Where is the bike?
Is it going to be worth travelling to the next county/state, or even across a border? A locally advertised machine, although it may not sound very interesting, can add to your knowledge for very little effort, so make a visit – it might even be in better condition than expected.

Dealer or private sale
Establish early on if the bike is being sold by its owner or by a trader. A private owner should have all the history, so don't be afraid to ask detailed questions. A dealer may have more limited knowledge of the bike's history, but should have some documentation. A dealer may offer a warranty/guarantee (ask for a printed copy).

Cost of collection and delivery
A dealer may well be used to quoting for delivery. A private owner may agree to meet you halfway, but only agree to this after you have seen the bike at the vendor's address to validate the documents. Conversely, you could meet halfway and agree the sale, but insist on meeting at the vendor's address for the handover.

View – when and where
It is always preferable to view at the vendor's home or business premises. In the case of a private sale, the bike's documentation should tally with the vendor's name and address. Arrange to view only in daylight, and avoid a wet day – the vendor may be reluctant to let you take a test ride if it's wet.

Reason for sale
Do make it one of the first questions. Why is the bike being sold and how long has it been with the current owner? How many previous owners?

Condition
Ask for an honest appraisal of the bike's condition. Ask specifically about some of the check items described in Chapter 7.

All original specification
As BMW airheads are still quite plentiful, absolute originality isn't a big issue, at least not yet. The exceptions are the older /5s and /6s, and the R90S, which is still by far the most collectable of the flat-twins. Other later bikes, notably the R100RS and RT,

and possibly the R65LS, will join the collectable list as they become rarer in original form.

Matching data/legal ownership
Do frame, engine numbers and licence plate match the official registration document? Is the owner's name and address recorded in the official registration documents?

For those countries that require an annual test of roadworthiness, does the bike have a document showing it complies (an MoT certificate in the UK, which can be verified on 0845 600 5977)? In the UK, bikes registered in 1975 or earlier are exempt from VED (Vehicle Excise Duty, better known as 'road tax').

Does the vendor own the bike outright? Money might be owed to a finance company or bank: the bike could even be stolen. Several organisations will supply the data on ownership, based on the bike's licence plate number, for a fee. Such companies can often also tell you whether the bike has been 'written off' by an insurance company. In the UK these organisations can supply vehicle data:
HPI - 01722 422 422 – www.hpicheck.com
AA - 0870 600 0836 – www.theaa.com
RAC - 0870 533 3660 – www.rac.co.uk
Other countries will have similar organisations.

Unleaded fuel
With leaded fuel unavailable for many years now, many bikes will have been converted to use unleaded, or owners will use an additive. High compression engines may need an octane booster as well.

Insurance
Check with your existing insurer before setting out - your current policy might not cover you if you do buy the bike and decide to ride it home.

How you can pay
Electronic transfer via internet banking is the quickest means of paying, and avoids waiting for a cheque/check to clear. Some sellers still prefer good old-fashioned cash, or may not want to email their bank details to you. The most secure way to transfer details is verbally over the phone, with the buyer inputting them directly onto his/her internet banking screen.

Buying at auction?
If the intention is to buy at auction see Chapter 10 for further advice.

Professional vehicle check (mechanical examination)
There are often marque/model specialists who will undertake professional examination of a bike on your behalf. Owners' clubs may be able to put you in touch with such specialists.

6 Inspection equipment

– these items will really help

Inspection equipment
This book
Reading glasses (if you need them for close work)
Overalls
Camera/smartphone
Compression tester
A friend, preferably a knowledgeable enthusiast

Before you rush out of the door, gather together a few items that will help as you work your way around the bike. This book is designed to be your guide at every step, so take it along and use the check boxes to help you assess each area of the bike you're interested in. Don't be afraid to let the seller see you using it.

Take your reading glasses if you need them to read documents and make close up inspections.

Be prepared to get dirty. Take along a pair of overalls if you have them, and a camera or smartphone, so that later you can study some areas of the bike more closely. Take a picture of any part of the bike that causes you concern, and seek a friend's opinion.

A compression tester is easy to use. It screws into the sparkplug holes, easy to get to on the Boxers. With the engine warm and both spark plugs removed, turn the engine over on the starter on full throttle to get the compression reading – the correct reading will take 5-6 turns of the engine. 120-160psi is acceptable, but 100psi or less suggests a worn top end (pistons/rings, valve wear etc). There is likely to be a difference in reading between the two cylinders, but this shouldn't be more than 20psi.

Ideally, have a friend or knowledgeable enthusiast accompany you: a second opinion is always valuable.

7 Fifteen minute evaluation
– walk away or stay?

Engine/frame numbers

Engine and frame numbers are mentioned several times in this book, with good reason. They are unique to the bike, a good means of checking whether the documentation actually relates to the bike and whether the engine and frame are original.

The engine number is on a raised boss underneath the left-hand cylinder barrel, the frame number stamped on the right hand lower frame rail, and there may also be a number stamped on a plate fasted to the right-hand of the head stock. Any 'fuzzy' numbers could be a sign of tampering, and if there is, or the numbers don't agree with those on the paperwork, look for another bike.

For a fuller explanation of engine/frame numbers, see page 23, and for a full rundown of engine numbers by model and year, see pages 57-59.

Put the bike on its centre stand and have a good look round ...

Documentation

If the seller claims to be the bike's owner, make sure he/she really is by checking the registration document, which in the UK is V5C. The person listed on the V5C isn't necessarily the legal owner, but their details should match those of whoever is selling the bike. Also check that the engine/frame numbers on the V5C are the same as those on the bike.

An annual roadworthiness certificate – the 'MoT' in the UK – is not only handy proof that the bike was roadworthy when tested, but, if there's a whole sheaf of them, also gives evidence of the bike's history – when it was actively being used, and what the mileage was. The more of these that come with the bike, the better.

Also in the UK, motorcycles built over 40 years ago do not have to pay road fund tax – this is a rolling programme, which extends the exemption on 1st April each year. As this book went to press BMW boxers built before 1st January 1976 qualified.

Documents must match the bike.

Beware upgraded bikes

Many classic bikes are in danger of being faked – that is, a 'cooking' model dressed up to be something far more valuable. The only BMW airhead that fits into this category is the highly collectible R90S, and it is, in theory, possible to add a few parts to a cheaper R90/6 and pass it off as an S. Unfortunately, the engine number isn't much help because both bikes share the same first two digits ('49' for US market bikes; '40' for everywhere else), but the frame numbers do differentiate between R90/6 and R90S (see page 57).

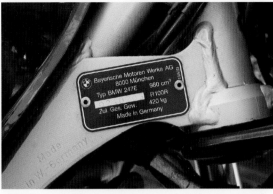

Check engine/frame numbers against the paperwork.

In practice, it should be easy to spot a fake as there are several features unique to the R90S, and it would be difficult to replicate them all – see pages 57-59 for a rundown of what these are.

General condition

Put the bike on its centre stand, to shed equal light on both sides, and take a good, slow walk around it. If it's claimed to be restored, and has a nice shiny tank and engine cases, look more closely – how far does the 'restored' finish go? Are the nooks and crannies behind the gearbox as spotless as the fuel tank? If not, the bike may have been given a quick smarten-up to sell. A generally faded look all over isn't necessarily a bad thing – it suggests a machine that hasn't been restored, and isn't trying to pretend that it has.

Now look at the engine – by far the most expensive and time-consuming thing to put right if anything's wrong. Take the bike off the centre stand and start the engine. Don't be alarmed by blue smoke from the left-hand pot – they all do that if left on the sidestand for a while, as oil drains down into that cylinder, and should soon burn off. Once running, the engine should rev crisply and cleanly without showing blue or black smoke. There will be some top end noise, but listen for rumbles and knocks from the bottom end – if a rumble goes away when the clutch is held in, it's likely to be the gearbox bearings. While the engine's running, check that the oil and charge lights have gone off.

Switch off the engine and put the bike back on its centre stand. Check for play in the forks, headstock and swingarm, and check the front forks or rear shocks for leaks.

Are the bolt or screw heads chewed or rounded-off? Is there damage to casings around bolt heads? Has someone attacked fixings with a hammer and chisel? All are sure signs of a careless previous owner with more enthusiasm than skill, coupled with a dash of youthful impatience. No one has tried to butcher this nut & bolt though.

On the test ride, listen for rumbling from the gearbox. If serious it means one or all of the six bearings are on their way out, which is of course a gearbox out job. It's a tricky call though – some gearboxes can carry on for several years if the noise isn't too bad. If in doubt, don't buy.

Check for oil leaks between the engine and gearbox. If the rear main oil seal has failed, the gearbox will have to be removed to replace it. This misting around the cylinder base hardly counts as a leak.

Centre stands can wear and collapse, partly because the BMW is no lightweight, partly because the spring-loaded side stand is awkward to use, so the centre stand gets a lot use – many owners have fitted more positive side stands like the Surefoot.

Alloy wheels are vulnerable to damage, so check these for dents, dings and cracks. BMW did run a recall on pre-1982 19-inch front wheels, which could crack between the hub and alloy spokes, but it's possible a bike may have missed this. The R45 and R65 (18-inch wheel) weren't covered by the recall.

9 Serious evaluation
– 30 minutes for years of enjoyment

Circle the Excellent (4), Good (3), Average (2) or Poor (1) box of each section as you go along. The totting up procedure is detailed at the end of the chapter. Be realistic in your marking!

Engine/frame numbers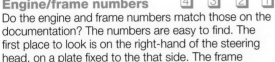

Do the engine and frame numbers match those on the documentation? The numbers are easy to find. The first place to look is on the right-hand of the steering head, on a plate fixed to the that side. The frame number is stamped on top of the right-hand lower frame rail and the engine number on a raised boss in the crankcase, just below the left-hand cylinder barrel. The numbers may be difficult to spot on an RT, being obscured by the fairing.

Engine number on raised boss below left-hand cylinder.

In each case, check the numbers against any documents you have, and also that the numbers are clearly stamped and not fuzzy – they may have been tampered with, and if that's the case, or the numbers don't agree with the paperwork, then walk away. There are plenty of legitimate BMW boxers around, so there's no need to risk buying something with an uncertain history.

Check plate riveted to headstock.

All twin-shock bikes – that is, everything built up to 1984 – have matching engine and frame numbers, and if the bike you're looking at has those, it's evidence that the engine and frame are the originals. If not, either the engine or frame has been changed at some point. There can be good reasons for this, and the bike may still be perfectly serviceable, but not being original will depress the value a little. The first two digits of the engine number denote the model, and the other numbers are the sequential production number.

Monoshock bikes (1985 model year onwards) – use a different system. The engine/frame numbers don't match, but the engine number can tell you which week the engine was built in: the first two digits denote

Frame number stamped on right-hand lower frame tube.

the week, the second two the number and the final four, the sequential number in that week's production. So 12/91/0250 refers to the 12th week of production in 1991 model year, the 250th engine built that week.

VIN (Vehicle Identification Numbers) were phased in over 1980-82.

See pages 57-59 for a complete listing of engine numbers by model and year.

Paint, chrome & alloy

BMW quality has such a reputation that it can lead to a false sense of security. The fact is that the youngest airhead is now over 20 years old and inevitably time

Once corrosion creeps underneath lacquer the results are ugly – this is an oilhead 1150GS, but the results are the same.

Chrome was good quality when new, but requires attention to keep it that way.

New decals are available.

Paintwork generally lasts well.

takes its toll. There's nothing magical about the legendary BMW finish, and eventually even garaged bikes will suffer from dull chrome, bubbling alloy and rust. That said, the paint quality is good and doesn't seem vulnerable to fading, though it does tend to rub off between the fuel tank and seat. The frame in particular will suffer, and it's worth checking the section just in front of the rear mudguard, where the frame can be sprayed by a mixture of water, grit, salt and dirt – check the battery carrier and the front of the rear subframe.

On later bikes the crankcase alloy is coated in lacquer, which looks great when new, but once moisture gets underneath the alloy begins to bubble up as corrosion takes hold. Check all over the engine, but especially at the front where it's vulnerable to spray from the front wheel – if the owner has fitted a mudguard extension or a crud plate, that's a good sign. Damaged lacquer is a purely cosmetic problem, but it doesn't look good, and could be a lever to reduce the price of the whole bike.

Tinwork & fibreglass

There is no metal bodywork on a BMW airhead – from the very first /5 the mudguards were fibreglass, as were sidepanels fitted from 1972. But all the fuel tanks are steel, and eventually these can leak. Check the underside for signs of weeping or staining, and if it's oily, this may be the factory protective coating seeping out through pinholes. BMW was one of the few manufacturers to rustproof the inside of its fuel tanks.

Not all fairing panels are still available, so check them for cracking and other damage.

Headlight fairing fitted to R90S, R100S and CS.

Tanks can often be repaired, and minor weeps can be cured with an off-the-shelf sealant. If the damage is too bad, new tanks aren't available. However, as airheads are still around in big numbers, poor condition bikes are being broken up, so used tanks (and plenty of other parts) can still be sourced. BMW only made a few styles of tank, so it is possible to find the correct one, though you'll be lucky if it's in the right colour!

RT and RS fairings are more of a challenge, though these, too, are sometimes available secondhand. As more RTs and RSs are stripped of their fairings to build custom bikes, this could

All mudguards are fibreglass.

be the time to buy a spare, as they won't be available for ever. Check the fairing for cracked or damaged panels, especially the lower right-hand panel on the R100RS, which has to be removed to reach the oil filter but can be pried off by mechanics in a hurry. Fairing screens will eventually become crazed and discoloured, but new ones are available.

Finally, while at the front of the bike, does the bike have crashbars? If so, check for dents and scrapes to indicate that the bike really has had a smash – the crashbars will have protected the engine, but if there is evidence of a crash, look elsewhere for further damage.

Seat ④ ③ ② ①

BMW airhead seats are substantial items with (early R100RS apart) plenty of room for two – most were black as standard, but there are some specials, such as the all-white seat fitted to some R100RTs. Early seat bases were metal, so these need to be checked for rust, which in an extreme case could collapse – later glassfibre or plastic bases don't suffer from that. Also check that the seat hinges (just a hook and a pin) have the tiny retaining washers that keep the seat place.

This RT seat has been repaired with tape, otherwise it's okay.

Seat covers can split, and once they start to go they only get worse, letting in the rain which the seat foam soaks up – it's a recipe for a permanently wet backside. Any seat can be recovered by a specialist (though it is possible to do a DIY job) which is worth doing if you are planning on keeping the bike.

Cracks in the seat, just visible here, will swallow water.

Is the seat base undamaged?

Footrest/kickstart rubbers

⁴ ³ ² ¹

Worn footrest rubbers, or very new ones, are a good sign of high mileage, and should have the BMW logo moulded into them. Hardly a deal breaker, but seriously worn rubbers could have your feet slipping off, and they are a sign of owner neglect. If the rubber is torn or the footrest itself is bent upwards, that's an indication of crash damage.

Check footrests for splits and wear.

Frame

⁴ ³ ² ¹

All BMW airheads used a simple and strong tubular steel frame, with oval tubing – the top tube was single-skinned on the R45/R65, double on everything else. It consists of a welded front half, which supports the engine, gearbox and steering head, and a bolted-on rear subframe for the seat and swingarm. The subframe can crack on early /5s, where the rear light wires pass through a drilled hole – this is behind the rear shock mounting, so it's not a safety issue, but worth checking anyway.

It's important to check whether the entire frame is straight and true. Crash damage may have bent it, putting the wheels out of line. One way of checking is an experienced eye, some string and a straight edge, but the surest way to ascertain a frame's straightness is on the test ride – any serious misalignment should be obvious in the way the bike handles. If the wheels are out of line, it will try and drift to one side rather than run straight.

A really shabby frame necessitates a strip down

Tubular frame in all its glory.

The rear subframe is bolted onto the main frame.

and repaint, though, as with the other paintwork, if it's original and fits with the patina of the bike, then there's a good case for leaving it as it is.

Look for bent brackets, which can be heated and bent back into shape, and cracks around them, which can be welded.

Stands

These are heavy bikes, and the stands can take some punishment – the centre stand shouldn't allow the bike to wobble, and should keep front or rear wheel off the ground. The flip-up sidestand is one of the bike's most awkward features, needing to be held down against the springs while allowing the bike's weight to rest onto it. Many owners fit a non-flip stand such as the Surefoot, which bolts straight on.

Centre stand should be solid and secure.

Original, and the more substantial Surefoot sidestands.

Lights

BMW lights are good, standard 12-volt items, but check that the headlight reflector isn't tarnished or corroded, both of which are an MoT failure in the UK. Replacement reflectors and headlight glasses are available. Blown rear bulbs can be replaced quite cheaply with LED bulbs, which won't blow.

Extra spotlights are a common fitment.

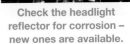

Check the headlight reflector for corrosion – new ones are available.

Electrics/wiring

The Bosch electrical system is of good quality and pretty reliable, though it's vulnerable to all the usual problems with elderly electrics – corroded connectors, poor earths, and tired switchgear. The nice thing is that the wiring loom is very logically laid out, with numbered terminals and multi-pin connectors, so it's easier to

Charge light (middle red one) should come on with the ignition and go off when the engine starts.

Twin six-volt coils live under the fuel tank (packing is non-standard).

The general state of the wiring is a good indicator of electrical health, but not much of it is visible.

trace the wiring through than on some classic bikes. It's also a fairly simple and straightforward system with contact breaker points (electronic ignition from 1981), an ignition control unit, and voltage regulator.

Occasional odd faults could be down to corrosion on the printed circuit board found inside the headlight – also check the board's copper connectors, and look for any resoldered joints. Electrical faults often arise from home conversions – extra spotlights are a favourite, mounted on the crashbars. Early /5s had no fuses, but most will have had them (or at least one) fitted since.

Check that everything works and that the wiring you can see is tidy, though most of it is hidden under the tank. It's crucial that the alternator is charging correctly – the charge light should come on when the ignition is switched on, and if it doesn't this suggests alternator failure (don't believe the seller who insists 'it's just the bulb.') The light should go out as soon as the engine starts and reaches a fast idle. If you have access to the alternator, check it with a multimeter – an infinite high resistance reading confirms it has failed.

The charge rate is controlled by the voltage regulator under the tank – mechanical on early bikes, electronic on later ones – and the electronic box is a direct retro fit. Some specialists offer a high-output electronic regulator, as used by police machines. This boosts output at low revs, which is useful for urban commuters.

Corrosion can affect the various connectors and components under the tank, which includes the twin six-volt coils fitted to early bikes. 1984-92 bikes, plus all post-1981 R45/65s, used a double-ended coil, which doesn't have the best reputation. Failure is signalled by poor cold starting and intermittent running, often caused by a cracked plastic casing. The replacement coil (Bosch part no 0.221.500.203) is a direct replacement. Pre-1981 R45/65s can also fracture the front coil bracket, which, as it carries the main earth connection, causes complete electric failure. Specialists recommend fitting an extra earth cable between the coil bracket and the main frame.

Wiring joints that appear to be soldered are actually crimped – water can collect inside the outer sheath and cause corrosion, and hence strange, apparently unconnected faults. As with all electrics, the most you can do on examining the bike is check that everything works, that the engine fires up promptly, and that the alternator is charging – and quiz the owner as to what (if anything) has been replaced.

Wheels/tyres

4️⃣ 3️⃣ 2️⃣ 1️⃣

Three types of wheels are fitted to BMW airheads: conventional spoked wheels with tubed tyres, alloy wheels, and external spoked wheels for tubeless tyres, fitted to the final R100Rs. To examine the wheels, put the bike on its centre stand and spin each wheel slowly.

On all spoked wheels, check for loose spokes (give each one a tap with screwdriver – any 'off-key' will need retensioning) and on the R90 for cracks around the spoke holes – cracks mean rim replacement. Alloy wheels can dent, especially at the front, but more serious is

Tyres on bikes unused for a long time may have hardened or cracked.

Check alloy wheels for cracks and dents.

possible cracking between the hub and spokes. Pre-1982 bikes with 19-inch front alloy wheels were subject to a recall because of this, but that didn't include the 18-inch wheel on R45/65s, which can still crack.

On all wheels, spin them faster to check they are not running out of true – anything visible is suspect, as the UK MoT allows only 2mm runout.

Tyres should have at least the legal minimum of tread. In the UK that's 1mm of tread depth across three-quarters of the breadth of the tyre. Or, if the tread doesn't reach that far across the breadth (true of some modern tyres), then any tread showing must be

Corrosion can be just cosmetic, as long as spokes and rim are solid.

at least 1mm deep. Beware of bikes that have been left standing (especially on the sidestand) for some time, allowing the tyres to crack and deteriorate – it's no reason to reject the bike, but a good lever to reduce the price.

Wheel bearings

④ ③ ② ①

Unusually, pre-1985 BMW airheads (except the R65LS) have taper-roller wheel bearings – the advantage is that some play can be adjusted out, though the bearings do need to have just the right amount of pre-load, which involves shimming them accurately.

/5 bearings can come loose in the hub, which is bad news, as the only cure is removing the hub, machining the hub out and resleeving it. On twin-shock bikes, it's usually the nearside rear bearing which fails first, as the seal is exposed to grit.

A wheel bearing check is easy to do – there should be no play.

Whether the bike has taper-roller or ball bearings, to check the front wheel bearings, put the bike on its centre stand, put the steering on full lock, and try rocking the front wheel in a vertical plane, then spin the wheel and listen for signs of roughness. Do the same for the rear wheel in a horizontal plane. If the bearings do need replacing, try to find sealed replacements, which will last longer.

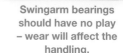

Swingarm bearings should have no play – wear will affect the handling.

Swing arm bearings ④ ③ ② ①

Another essential for good handling is the swing arm bearings, and again these are taper-rollers. To check for wear, get hold of the rear wheel (or on twin-shock bikes, the swingarm itself) and try rocking the complete swing arm from side to side, feeling for any movement at the pivot. There should be nothing perceptible, but if there is, haggle on the price, as replacement is a difficult job which requires removing the swingarm complete.

Steering head bearings ④ ③ ② ①

Like the wheel bearings, these are taper-rollers, underlining the point that these bikes were built to a higher standard than many rivals, especially in the 1970s. However, airheads are sensitive to badly adjusted steering head bearings.

Check the taper-roller steering head bearings – again, any play will spoil the handling.

Put the bike on its centre stand, and with the front wheel off the ground allow the bars to drop to left or right lock – the bearings should be free enough to allow the forks to fall under their own weight, and without a hint of roughness or stiff patches. To check for play, put the front brake on hard and attempt to rock the bike back and forth – there should be none. The front fork check (see below) may also highlight steering head play.

Suspension ④ ③ ② ①

Airheads are renowned for their soft, long travel suspension, but, apart from the Boge Nivomat self-levelling shocks fitted to early RTs, it's a very conventional setup. On pre-1985 bikes, you get non-adjustable telescopic forks plus twin rear shocks with pre-load adjustment. With 1985-on Monoshocks, the difference is a single pre-load adjustable shock, rather than two.

Check the forks and rear shock/s for leaks. Many airheads have fork gaiters, but it's worth rubbing the gaiter against the stanchion – if it moves very easily, there could be oil

All early bikes (R90S excepted) have fork gaiters.

Monoshock rear end, with distinctive bulge in side cover to accommodate the shock.

Check the shocks for leaks, and damping on the test ride.

Checking for fork play.

underneath. Likewise, gaiters will protect stanchions from pitting and corrosion, but time takes its toll, especially on bikes stored in damp conditions. Pump the forks up and down – they shouldn't feel 'saggy,' and should travel their full length without any clonks. To check for play, put the bike on its centre stand, grasp the bottom of the forks, and try to rock them back and forth – there shouldn't be any play, but if there is it can be confused with play at the steering head bearings. There shouldn't be any of that either, of course.

Testing the rear shocks really has to wait for the test ride, and if that shows they have lost their damping, allowing the bike to bounce on the spring, replacements are available: either Hagons or IKON, which are the modern equivalent of the old Koni Dial-A-Ride shocks.

Early RTs were fitted with Boge Nivomat shocks, which automatically pumped up to match the load, whether it was a solo rider or two-up with a pile of luggage. Shrouded by a rubber bellows, they are easily identifiable. Unfortunately, Nivomats aren't available any more and cannot be rebuilt, so if they aren't pumping

Wear on underside of rear mudguard indicates previous overloading.

up, they will have to be replaced with a conventional shock.

Finally, have a look at the front underside of the rear mudguard – if it's worn, that's an indication the bike has done lots of heavily-laden miles, as the rear suspension travel can allow the tyre to hit the mudguard on full rebound.

The /6 instruments – /5s had combined speedo and rev counter.

Instruments

/5s have a combined speedo/rev counter – the rev counter needle often flutters, and apparently it's

inherent. If a 5/ speedo
needle is fluttering,
that's more indicative
that the head is about
to fail. New heads are
available, but should
be matched to the final
drive ratio (marked on
the head) for an accurate
reading. The same goes
for the separate speedo/
rev counters fitted to all

R45/65 warning lights
(apart from indicators) are
in the rev counter.

Full set of instruments
with voltmeter and clock
on an R100RT.

other airheads. While looking at the speedo, remember that 50,000 miles could be
150,000, or even 250,000! However, genuine low mileage airheads do still come up.

Engine/gearbox – general impression ④ ③ ② ①

BMW airhead flat-twins are relatively
simple and in some ways easy to work
on, although over the years this does
encourage some keen owners to take
things apart, sometimes without the
proper tools or knowledge. Look for
chewed up screw or allen bolt heads,
or rounded off bolts, plus damage to
the casings around them.

Have a good look round the engine for
leaks, cracked hoses or signs of neglect.

Also check for crash damage –
there's no getting away from the fact
that those horizontal cylinders are
more vulnerable than an in-line engine.
Do the rocker covers have scrapes or
dents, and are any fins on the head
broken? If there are crashbars, do
these show signs of being bashed or
scraped?

Pull the dipstick out (on the
left-hand side) and check the oil for
metallic particles, which could be a
sign of cam followers breaking up on
early engines, or other mechanical
wear. The good news is that airheads
are not prone to oil leaks, because of
good build quality, few mating joints
and decent gaskets. Misting at the
cylinder barrel base can happen, but
it does no harm and isn't common in
any case.

Are the carb hoses in place, and in good
condition?

Look underneath the engine – a leak near the rear could mean the main bearing
oil seal has failed, or that a worn top end is causing blow back, or it could just be
the sump gasket, which is easy to replace. While underneath, have a look at the

pushrod tube seals, as eventually these will harden and start to leak. Oil inside the front timing cover (which you'll only know about if looking at a partially stripped engine) suggests camshaft wear, which allows oil through from behind the cb points plate.

Any signs of crash damage on the rocker covers?

Scrapes and dents on the crash bars (if fitted) are more evidence of crash damage.

Check where the speedo drive cable enters the gearbox vertically on the right-hand side. If the rubber seal is perished it can allow water into the box, damaging the nearest bearing over time.

The carburettors can suffer from leaking float bowl gaskets, perished mounting rubbers and tired diaphragms – some say the latter should be replaced periodically, so ask a long-term owner

Check the pushrod tubes underneath the cylinders for leaks.

when this was last done. Stromberg carburettor diaphragms are cheaper than the genuine Bings, but a direct replacement.

Check the clutch operating pivot on the back of the gearbox. The casting in which the pivot pin runs can wear, which is difficult and expensive to repair. It should be well greased, and there shouldn't be any play in the pin.

Finally, though it's not specific to the engine and gearbox, early bikes had several grease nipples. Do these look clean, with a smear of fresh grease on top? That's a good sign, but a nipple covered in dirt which clearly hasn't seen a grease gun for a long time indicates a neglectful owner.

Engine – starting/idling

If possible, try to give the bike a cold start test, which gives the battery and starter motor a good work out, especially first thing in the morning. Don't forget that all airheads have a manual choke.

The starter motor should engage without graunching (though clonks are normal), and settle down to a steady idle. If it won't idle evenly after a minute or so of warming up, it could just be carburettor or valve adjustment required, or possibly the carbs require a service (usually every 10,000 miles). Rough running can also be caused by the points assembly

Thumb the green button – the engine should start without the starter motor graunching.

coming loose, sometimes caused by the mounting bolt being overtightened, stripping the thread and allowing the plate to loosen.

There's always a possibility that poor idling could be down to valve seat recession, especially on 1980-84 bikes; obviously a more serious problem than any adjustments, though replacing the valve seats is relatively easy.

Engine – smoke/noise

The good news is that BMW flat-twins, if you hadn't got the message yet, are extremely robust, long-lived engines, especially by motorcycle standards. Given regular oil/filter changes, they should have little trouble reaching six-figure mileages without major bottom end work. The top end will wear eventually, but worn crankshafts are quite rare.

Don't be alarmed by a cloud of blue smoke from the left-hand cylinder on starting up. This is very common, caused when the bike has been left on its sidestand, which allows oil to drain down into that cylinder, even if the pistons and bores are in good condition. It should burn off quite quickly.

These engines are fairly quiet mechanically, though there will be some slight chattering from the valve gear. If there's a lot of top end clatter,

A fresh oil leak underneath an R100 – it could be from the rear main bearing seal.

Don't be put off by blue smoke from the left-hand pot from a cold start – it should burn off. This is a Triumph, but BMW blue smoke is the same!

With the engine idling, pull in the clutch – any pronounced change in gearbox noise?

the needle-roller rocker arm bearings may have broken – /5s used plain rocker arm bushes, which just wear. A more noticeable tapping could be the tappets or a worn timing chain, the latter easy to replace behind the front timing cover – it's good practice to replace the tensioners at the same time, as these will keep the new chain quiet for longer.

Assuming any start-up blue smoke has dissipated, look back at the silencers and blip the throttle. Blue smoke means the engine is burning oil and is a sign of general wear in the top end, with pistons/rings and valves/guides the culprits. That usually means a rebore, and parts, including oversize pistons, are available. Black smoke, indicating rich running, is less of a problem, caused by carburettor wear.

If it's blue smoke, it may be just the piston rings which require replacing; often needed at 60-70,000 miles. Valve guides do wear, and if not replaced they force the valves to run lopsidedly, which can eventually cause the valve head to drop off – the safe option is to replace the guides at 50,000 miles. R45/65s seem to suffer from a higher rate of valve and guide wear than the bigger twins.

As mentioned, serious bottom end wear is quite rare, but do listen for knocking when the engine is under load – it's easier to detect on the rest ride than when just blipping the throttle at a standstill. Finally, listen for gearbox noise – if there's a pronounced rushing/rumbling sound which stops when the clutch is pulled in, then one or more of the gearbox bearings is worn.

Shaft/final drive

Shaft drive does cut down on maintenance compared to a chain, but there is some to do, and eventually the shaft and final drive will wear. With the bike on its centre stand, and the engine off and in first gear, try rocking the rear wheel back and forth – about an inch or so of movement is normal, but any more indicates wear – an

overhaul is a specialist job, and sometimes a good secondhand unit from one of the specialists could be cheaper. On the test ride, listen for loud whining on acceleration or the overrun, more evidence of wear. However, this is rare, and with regular oil changes the final drive is very long lasting. The drive splines between final drive and rear wheel should have been greased regularly, so ask when this was last done.

These driveshaft bellows are fine ... but can you spot the seriously cracked bolt housing?

Pre-1988 bikes (twin-shock and Monolever) have one universal joint in the driveshaft, and Paralevers (1988-on) have two. Play in the Paralever rear UJ and pivot bearing can be detected by placing a hand

Listen for whining from the bevel drive on acceleration and the overrun.

over the joint and trying to rock the rear wheel from side to side – any movement should be obvious. An audible clonk as the drive takes up is another sign of UJ wear on any bike – generally these are long-lived, though they can fail with little warning. On all bikes, check that the rubber bellows are in good condition without splits or tears.

Battery

The battery lives under the front of the seat.

Airheads need a good battery, especially the R90s and 100s. It's easily found under the nose of the seat, and a multimeter voltage check will indicate its general condition. Batteries aren't expensive, but replacing one on an early bike involves loosening the rear subframe before it can be manoeuvred out. If the bike has been laid up for a while, but the owner has kept the battery topped-up with a trickle charger, that's a good sign.

Exhaust

All airheads used a twin silencer system, with a collector box under the gearbox. The box is the first to corrode, so check underneath and give it a poke with a screwdriver. When it does go, many owners ditch the box and replace the whole

Check silencers and collector box for corrosion.

system with a two-into-one, which is lighter, if not original. If they've paid extra for a stainless steel system, that's a bonus.

Test ride
The test ride should be not less than 10 minutes, and you should be doing the riding – not the seller riding with you on the pillion. It's understandable that some sellers are reluctant to let a complete stranger loose on their pride and joy, but it does go with the territory

Any signs of leakage from any of the exhaust joints?

of selling a bike, and so long as you leave an article of faith (usually the vehicle you arrived in) then all should be happy. Take your driving licence in case the seller wants to see it.

Engine performance ④ ③ ② ①
If you've not ridden a BMW flat-twin before, be ready for the torque reaction

when blipping the throttle at a standstill. Generally, these are easy bikes to ride, well balanced and with tractable engines, but you just have to remember the weight, and if you're used to a four-cylinder bike, the big twin will seem lumpy at low revs, and less eager to run up to the red line, but that's normal.
    Whichever model it is, the

Lots of information can be gleaned on the test ride.

BMW airheads should be fun to ride (R80ST shown).

engine should pick up well from low revs and run up to 6-7000rpm fairly smoothly, without glitches or hiccups. These engines respond best in the mid-range and don't have to be ridden hard. A clicky, ratchet-like feel to the twistgrip indicates worn gears – unlike other bikes, airheads have a gear system for the throttle control. Misfiring once the engine is warm suggests that the coil (or one of them if it's an early bike with twin six-volt coils) is breaking down.

Clutch operation · 4 3 2 1

BMW clutches, like the engines, are long-lived, and can run for 60-80,000 miles, though this depends on riding style. Check the clutch isn't slipping, which is a sign of general wear or oil finding its way through the rear crankshaft seal or flywheel O-ring. Either way, it's a gearbox-out job which should be factored into the price. When replacing the clutch plate, the advice is to replace the related parts as well, including the diaphragm, so budget for those, too. A sudden take up of drive indicates that the input shaft is dry or needs shimming.

Gearbox operation · 4 3 2 1

We've already mentioned that BMW airheads have a slow and sometimes noisy gearchange, so don't worry about that, because they are all the same, though post-1983 bikes were improved. The important thing is that the gears engage cleanly, and that the bike doesn't jump out of gear on acceleration or the overrun. /6 five-speeds can get stuck in one gear if the selector spring breaks, and the only cure for that is a complete gearbox strip.

Listen out for gearbox bearing noise.

Now then: noise. There will be some whining in all gears except top, because those gears are straight-cut, but bearing noise can be more serious. The gears themselves are robust, but the six bearings in the gearbox can fail, which shows up as a rushing/rumbling sound – the same one you checked when the bike idling on its centre stand. Noise here could mean failure is on the way, but some boxes carry on like this for many miles – boxes can need work as early as 40,000 miles or as late as 90,000.

If in doubt about the state of the box, ask if you can drain the gearbox oil to check for metallic particles – many drain plugs are magnetic, and will catch the evidence. If there's 'mayonnaise' in the oil, then water has got into the gearbox (the speedo cable is the most likely culprit). Draining the oil can tell you a lot, but the owner may well say no!

Handling · 4 3 2 1

Contrary to popular belief, BMW airheads handle pretty well, and the horizontal pots do not unduly restrict cornering clearance. As mentioned above, these are not quick steering bikes, but if all is well they should be stable round bends, and cope with mid-corner bumps without wallowing or shaking. If the bike does feel excessively bouncy, then suspect worn out rear shocks or tired fork springs. There will be some fork dive on hard braking, but that goes with the territory of soft, long-travel forks.

Brakes

All BMW airheads have good brakes, well up to the performance of the bikes, with the exception of the R75/5's front drum. ATE disc brakes used up to 1981 have tapered pads, which need to be properly set up, and if braking is poor they could just need adjusting. The other peculiarity of the ATEs is the front brake master cylinder mounted under the fuel tank, instead of the usual handlebar mount, operated by a cable from the lever. It's a complicated system which needs a cable in good condition, and can lead to the fluid level being neglected – BMW did add a low level warning light, but it may not be working. 1981-on bikes used Brembo brakes, with a conventional handlebar-mounted master cylinder.

Whichever disc brake it has, use the test ride to check for braking power and a spongy lever feel – a little sponginess is expected from the long rubber brake hoses, though many owners fit aftermarket braided hose. Back at base, carefully examine the disc/s for wear, grooving and hairline cracks, which can affect early stainless steel discs.

Drum front brakes are adequate for the R50 and R60.

Brembo front discs were fitted to all bikes from 1981.

Check rear drum brake arm spindle for oil leaks.

Pre-1981 ATE master cylinder lives under the fuel tank.

The drum brakes work well, and are fairly trouble-free, but if later rear drums aren't working well, this could be down to oil from the bevel drive leaking onto the shoes. The brake arm is sealed with bushes and O-rings, which can allow oil either way, into the brake, or onto the outside of the drum.

Cables

All the control cables – brakes, clutch, throttle, choke – should work smoothly, without stiffness or jerking. Poorly lubricated, badly adjusted cables are an indication of general neglect, and the same goes for badly routed cables.

Switchgear

The switchgear is generally reliable, but over time suffers from general wear and moisture. Just check that it all works as it should – if it doesn't, that's a good reason to bargain over the price. New switch clusters are available.

Hard-to-pull cables are a sign of neglect.

The switchgear is reliable, but check it all works.

Luggage

BMW airheads come with hard luggage more often than any other bike, usually panniers, though some have a topbox as well. Krauser or the original BMW cases are good quality, and will add most value to the bike. If they're fitted, check that they open, close and lock cleanly, and there's no sign of water leaks inside. They should also clip/unclip from the frames easily.

BMW or Krauser luggage adds value to the bike.

Evaluation procedure

Add up the total points.
Score: 116 = excellent; 87 = good; 58 = average; 29 = poor. Bikes scoring over 81 will be completely usable and will require only maintenance and care to preserve condition. Bikes scoring between 29 and 59 will require some serious work (at much the same cost regardless of score). Bikes scoring between 60 and 80 will require very careful assessment of the necessary repair/restoration costs in order to arrive at a realistic value.

10 Auctions
– sold! Another way to buy your dream

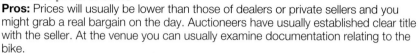

Auction pros & cons

Pros: Prices will usually be lower than those of dealers or private sellers and you might grab a real bargain on the day. Auctioneers have usually established clear title with the seller. At the venue you can usually examine documentation relating to the bike.

Cons: You have to rely on a sketchy catalogue description of condition & history. The opportunity to inspect is limited and you cannot ride the bike. Auction machines can be a little below par and may require some work. It's easy to overbid. There will usually be a buyer's premium to pay in addition to the auction hammer price.

Which auction?

Auctions by established auctioneers are advertised in the motorcycle magazines and on the auction houses' websites. A catalogue, or a simple printed list of the lots for auctions might only be available a day or two ahead, though often lots are listed and pictured on auctioneers' websites much earlier. Contact the auction company to ask if previous auction selling prices are available as this is useful information (details of past sales are often available on websites).

Catalogue, entry fee and payment details

When you purchase the catalogue of the bikes in the auction, it often acts as a ticket allowing two people to attend the viewing days and the auction. Catalogue details tend to be comparatively brief, but will include information such as 'one owner from new, low mileage, full service history,' etc. It will also usually show a guide price to give you some idea of what to expect to pay and will tell you what is charged as a 'Buyer's premium'. The catalogue will also contain details of acceptable forms of payment. At the fall of the hammer an immediate deposit is usually required, the balance payable within 24 hours. If the plan is to pay by cash there may be a cash limit. Some auctions will accept payment by debit card. Sometimes credit or charge cards are acceptable, but will often incur an extra charge. A bank draft or bank transfer will have to be arranged in advance with your own bank as well as with the auction house. No bike will be released before all payments are cleared. If delays occur in payment transfers then storage costs can accrue.

Buyer's premium

A buyer's premium will be added to the hammer price: don't forget this in your calculations. It's not usual for there to be a further state tax or local tax on the purchase price and/or on the buyer's premium.

Viewing

In some instances it's possible to view on the day or days before, as well as in the hours prior to, the auction. There are auction officials available who are willing to help out if need be. While the officials may start the engine for you, a test ride is out of the question. Crawling under and around the bike as much as you want is permitted. You can also ask to see any documentation available.

Bidding

Before you take part in the auction, decide your maximum bid – and stick to it!

It may take a while for the auctioneer to reach the lot you are interested in, so use that time to observe how other bidders behave. When it's the turn of your bike, attract the auctioneer's attention and make an early bid. The auctioneer will then look to you for a reaction every time another bid is made. Usually the bids will be in fixed increments until the bidding slows, when smaller increments will often be accepted before the hammer falls. If you want to withdraw from the bidding, make sure the auctioneer understands your intentions – a vigorous shake of the head when he or she looks to you for the next bid should do the trick!

Assuming that you are the successful bidder, the auctioneer will note your card or paddle number, and from that moment on you will be responsible for the bike.

If it is unsold, either because it failed to reach the reserve or because there was little interest, it may be possible to negotiate with the owner, via the auctioneers, after the sale is over.

Successful bid

There are two more items to think about – how to get the bike home, and insurance. If you can't ride it, your own or a hired trailer is one way, another is to have it shipped using the facilities of a local company. The auction house will also have details of companies specialising in the transport of bikes.

Insurance for immediate cover can usually be purchased on site, but it may be more cost-effective to make arrangements with your own insurance company in advance, and then call to confirm the full details.

eBay & other online auctions?

eBay & other online auctions once had a reputation for bargains, though many traders as well as private sellers now use eBay and prices have risen. As with any auction, the final price depends how many buyers are bidding and how desperately they want the bike!

Either way, it would be foolhardy to bid without examining the bike first, which is something most vendors encourage. A useful feature of eBay is that the geographical location of the bike is shown, so you can narrow your choices to those within a realistic radius of home. Be prepared to be outbid in the last few moments of the auction. Remember, your bid is binding and that it will be very, very difficult to get restitution in the case of a crooked vendor fleecing you – caveat emptor! Look at the seller's rating as well as the bike.

Be aware that some bikes offered for sale in online auctions are 'ghost' machines. Don't part with any cash without being sure that the vehicle does actually exist and is as described (usually pre-bidding inspection is possible).

Auctioneers

Barrett-Jackson www.barrett-jackson.com
British Car Auctions www.bca-europe.com
  or www.british-car-auctions.co.uk
Coys www.coys.co.uk
H&H www.classic-auctions.co.uk
Shannons www.shannons.com.au

Bonhams www.bonhams.com
Cheffins www.cheffins.co.uk
Christies www.christies.com
eBay www.ebay.com or www.ebay.co.uk
RM www.rmauctions.com
Silver www.silverauctions.com

11 Paperwork
– correct documentation is essential!

The paper trail
Older bikes sometimes come with a large portfolio of paperwork accumulated and passed on by a succession of proud owners. This documentation represents the real history of the machine, from which you can deduce how well it's been cared for, how much it's been used, which specialists have worked on it and the dates of major repairs and restorations. All of this information will be priceless to you as the new owner, so be very wary of bikes with little paperwork to support their claimed history.

Registration documents
All countries/states have some form of registration for private vehicles whether it's like the American 'pink slip' system or the British 'log book' system.

It is essential to check that the registration document is genuine, that it relates to the bike in question, and that all the details are correctly recorded, including frame and engine numbers (if these are shown). If you are buying from the previous owner, his or her name and address will be recorded in the document: this will not be the case if you are buying from a dealer.

In the UK the current (Euro-aligned) registration document is the V5C, and is printed in coloured sections of blue, green and pink. The blue section relates to the motorcycle specification, the green section has details of the registered keeper (who is not necessarily the legal owner) and the pink section is sent to the DVLA in the UK when the bike is sold. A small section in yellow deals with selling within the motor trade.

In the UK the DVLA will provide details of earlier keepers of the bike upon payment of a small fee, and much can be learned in this way.

If the bike has a foreign registration there may be expensive and time-consuming formalities to complete. Do you really want the hassle? Many BMW airheads were sold in Europe, North America and to a lesser extent Australasia, so you shouldn't have much trouble finding the bike you want without importing one.

However, if the bike you've set your heart on is abroad, you'll have to buy it sight unseen, and the paperwork involved in importing and re-registering is a daunting prospect. That means employing a shipping agent; you'll also have to budget in the shipping costs. Then there's (at the time of writing) 6% import duty on the bike and shipping costs, then 20% VAT on the whole lot. As there are plenty of airheads around in good condition, personally importing a bike doesn't look worthwhile.

Roadworthiness certificate
Most country/state administrations require that bikes are regularly tested to prove that they are safe to use on the public highway. In the UK that test (the 'MOT') is carried out at approved testing stations, for a fee. In the USA the requirement varies, but most states insist on an emissions test every two years as a minimum, while the police are charged with pulling over unsafe-looking vehicles.

In the UK the test is required on an annual basis for all post-1960 vehicles of more than three years old. Even if it isn't a legal necessity, a conscientious owner can opt to put the bike through the test anyway, as a health check. Of particular relevance for older bikes is that the certificate issued includes the mileage reading recorded at the test date and, therefore, becomes an independent record of that machine's history. Ask the seller if previous certificates are available. Without an MOT the bike should be trailered to its new home, unless you insist that a valid MOT is part of the deal. (Not such a bad idea this, as at least you will know the bike was roadworthy on the day it was tested and you don't need to wait for the old certificate to expire before having the test done.)

Road licence

The administration of every country/state charges some kind of tax for the use of its road system, the actual form of the 'road licence' and, how it is displayed, varying enormously country to country and state to state.

Whatever the form of the road licence, it must relate to the vehicle carrying it and must be present and valid if the bike is to be ridden on the public highway legally. The value of the license will depend on the length of time it will continue to be valid.

In the UK if a bike is untaxed because it has not been used for a period of time, the owner has to inform the licencing authorities, otherwise the vehicle's date-related registration number will be lost and there will be a painful amount of paperwork to get it re-registered. Also in the UK, bikes built before 1st January 1976 are road tax exempt, and this rolling exemption covers all bikes over 25 years, advancing each year. Bikes still had to display a valid paper disc until 1st October 2014, when these were abolished.

Certificates of authenticity

For many makes of older bike it is possible to get a certificate proving the age and authenticity (eg engine and frame numbers, paint colour and trim) of a particular machine. These are sometimes called 'Heritage Certificates' and if the bike comes with one of these it is a definite bonus. If you want to obtain one, the owners' club is the best starting point.

Valuation certificate

The vendor may have a recent valuation certificate, or letter signed by a recognised expert stating how much he, or she, believes the particular bike to be worth (such documents, together with photos, are usually needed to get 'agreed value' insurance). These should act only as confirmation of your own assessment of the bike rather than a guarantee of value as the expert has probably not seen it in the flesh. The easiest way to find out how to obtain a formal valuation is to contact the owners' club.

Service history

Airheads will often have been serviced at home by enthusiastic (and hopefully capable) owners for a good number of years. Nevertheless, try to obtain as much service history and other paperwork pertaining to the bike as you can. Naturally receipts from BMW specialists score most points in the value stakes. However, anything helps in the great authenticity game, items like the original bill of sale, handbook, parts invoices and repair bills adding to the story and the character of the machine. Even a brochure correct to the year of the bike's manufacture is a useful document, and something that you could well have to search hard to locate in future years. If the seller claims that the bike has been restored, then expect receipts and other evidence from a specialist restorer.

If the seller claims to have carried out regular servicing, ask what work was completed and when, and seek some evidence of it being carried out. Your assessment of the bike's overall condition should tell you whether the seller's claims are genuine.

Restoration photographs

If the seller tells you that the bike has been restored, then expect to be shown a series of photographs taken while the restoration was under way. Pictures taken at various stages, and from various angles, should help you gauge the thoroughness of the work. If you buy the bike, ask if you can have copies of all the photographs, as they form an important part of its history.

12 What's it worth?
– let your head rule your heart

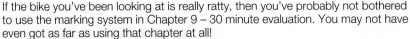

Condition

If the bike you've been looking at is really ratty, then you've probably not bothered to use the marking system in Chapter 9 – 30 minute evaluation. You may not have even got as far as using that chapter at all!

If you did use the marking system in Chapter 9 you'll know whether the bike is in Excellent (maybe concours), Good, Average or Poor condition or, perhaps, somewhere in-between these categories.

To keep up to date with prices, buy the latest editions of the classic bike magazines and check the classified and dealer ads, both in the magazines and online – these are particularly useful as they enable you to compare private and dealer prices. Most of the magazines run auction reports as well, which publish the actual selling prices, as do the auction house websites. Remember that the price listed for online auctions is only the highest current bid, not the final selling price (unless it's a 'Buy it Now' price).

BMW airheads are not 'blue chip' investments, but they are gradually increasing in value, and are very unlikely to depreciate in the near future. The R90S will always command a premium over everything else, but /5s and /6s will always hold their value, while the original R100RS and RT will become more valuable in years to come. The smaller R45, R65 and R80 are the cheapest route to airhead ownership, and should remain so. For each model, actual values depend more on condition than year or mileage.

Assuming that the bike you have in mind is not in show/concours condition, then relate the level of condition that you judge it to be in with the appropriate price in the adverts. How does the figure compare with the asking price?

Before you start haggling with the seller, consider what effect any variation from standard specification might have on the bike's value. This is a personal thing: for some, absolute originality is non-negotiable, while others see non-standard parts as an opportunity to pick up a bargain. Do your research in the reference books, so that you know the bike's spec when it left the factory. That way, you shouldn't end up paying a top-dollar price for a non-original bike. If you are buying from a dealer, remember prices are generally higher than in private sales.

Striking a deal

Negotiate on the basis of your condition assessment, mileage, and fault rectification cost. Also take into account the bike's specification. Be realistic about the value, but don't be completely intractable: a small compromise on the part of the vendor or buyer will often facilitate a deal at little real cost.

13 Do you really want to restore?

– it'll take longer and cost more than you think

There's a romance about restoration projects, about bringing a sick bike back into blooming health, and it's tempting to buy something that 'just needs a few small jobs' to bring it up to scratch. But there are two things to think about: one, once you've got the bike home and start taking it apart, those few small jobs could turn into big ones. Two, restoration takes time, which is a precious thing in itself. Be honest with yourself – will you get as much pleasure from working on the bike as you will from riding it?

A good restoration project? If you can find the missing parts.

Of course, you could hand over the whole lot to a professional, and the biggest cost involved there is not the new parts, but the sheer labour involved. Such restorations don't come cheap, and if taking this route there are a few other issues to bear in mind.

First, make it absolutely clear what you want doing. Do you want the bike to be 100% original at the end of the process, or simply

If you're not fussy about originality, this could be a bargain.

useable? Do you want a concours finish, or are you prepared to put up with a few blemishes on the original parts?

Second, make sure that not only is a detailed estimate involved, but that it is more or less binding. There are too many stories of a person quoted one figure only to be presented with an invoice for a far larger one!

Third, check that the company you're dealing with has a good reputation –

the owners' club, or one of the reputable parts suppliers, should be able to make a few recommendations.

Finally, a ground up restoration of any airhead, apart from an R90S or possibly a /5 or /6, could end up costing more than the finished bike will be worth. Not that this should put you off, if you have the budget, and really want to do it this way.

Living with this sort of corrosion is part of a running restoration.

Restoring the bike yourself requires a number of skills, which is fine if you already have them, but if you haven't it's good not to make your newly acquired bike part of the learning curve! Can you weld? Are you confident about building up an engine? Do you have a warm, well-lit garage with a solid workbench and good selection of tools?

Complete and original R100RT, but needing a lot of cosmetic work to make it concours.

Be prepared for a top-notch professional to put you on a lengthy waiting list or, if tackling a restoration yourself, expect things to go wrong and set aside extra time to complete the task. Restorations can stretch into years when things like life intrude, so it's good to have some sort of target date.

There's a lot to be said for a rolling restoration, especially as the summers start to pass with your airhead still off the road. This is not the way to achieve a concours finish, which can only really be achieved via a thorough nut-and-bolt rebuild, without the bike getting wet and gritty in the meantime, but an 'on-the-go' restoration does have its plus points. Riding helps keep your interest up as the bike's condition improves, and it's also more affordable than trying to do everything in one go. In the long run, it will take longer, but you'll get some on-road fun out of the bike in the meantime.

14 Paint problems
– bad complexion, including dimples, pimples and bubbles

Paint faults generally occur due to lack of protection/maintenance, or to poor preparation prior to a respray or touch-up. Some of the following conditions may be present in the bike you're looking at:

Light fuel stains should polish out.

Orange peel
This appears as an uneven paint surface, similar to the appearance of the skin of an orange. The fault is caused by the failure of atomised paint droplets to flow into each other when they hit the surface. It's sometimes possible to rub out the effect with proprietary paint cutting/rubbing compound or very fine grades of abrasive paper. A respray may be necessary in severe cases. Consult a paint shop for advice.

Cracking
Severe cases are likely to have been caused by too heavy an application of paint (or filler beneath the paint). Also, insufficient stirring of the paint before application can lead to the components being improperly mixed, and cracking can result. Incompatibility with the paint already on the panel can have a similar effect. To rectify it is necessary to rub down to a smooth, sound finish before respraying the problem area.

Crazing
Sometimes the paint takes on a crazed rather than a cracked appearance when the problems mentioned under 'cracking' are present. This problem can also be caused by a reaction between the underlying surface and the paint. Paint removal and respraying the problem area is usually the only solution.

The only cure for crazing is a repaint, but maybe you can live with it?

Blistering
Almost always caused by corrosion of the metal beneath the paint. Usually

perforations will be found in the metal and the damage will often be worse than that suggested by the area of blistering. The metal will have to be repaired before repainting.

Micro blistering
Usually the result of an economy respray where inadequate heating has allowed moisture to settle on the vehicle before spraying. Consult a paint specialist, but damaged paint will have to be removed before partial or full respraying. Can also be caused by bike covers that don't 'breathe.'

No problem here – beautifully repainted and restriped tank on an R60.

Fading
Some colours, especially reds, are pone to fading if subject to strong sunlight for long periods without the benefit of polish protection. Sometimes proprietary paint restorers and/or paint cutting/rubbing compounds will retrieve the situation. Often a respray is the only real solution.

Peeling
Often a problem with metallic paintwork when the sealing lacquer becomes damaged and begins to peel off. Poorly applied paint may also peel. The remedy is to strip and start again.

Dimples
Dimples in the paintwork are caused by the residue of polish (particularly silicone types) not being removed properly before respraying. Paint removal and repainting is the only solution.

Some parts cry out for repainting, but underneath it all this bike is perfectly serviceable.

15 Problems due to lack of use
– just like their owners, Boxers need exercise!

Like any piece of engineering, and indeed like human beings, BMW airheads deteriorate if they sit doing nothing for long periods. This is especially relevant if the bike is laid up for six months of the year, as some are.

Rust

If the bike is put away wet, and/or stored in a cold, damp garage, the paint, metal and brightwork will suffer. Ensure the machine is completely dry and clean before going into storage, and spray with an anti-corrosion oil. If you can afford it, invest in a dehumidifier to keep the garage atmosphere dry.

Cables

Cables are vulnerable to seizure – the answer is to thoroughly lube them beforehand, and give them a couple of pulls once a week or so.

Rubber parts crack – these driveshaft bellows are fine, but the cable seal on the right is on the way out.

Even the best quality switchgear will succumb to moisture, eventually.

Tyres

If the bike's been left on its sidestand, most of its weight is on the tyres, which will develop flat spots and cracks over time. Always leave the bike on its centre stand, which takes weight off the tyres.

Engine

Old, acidic oil can corrode bearings. Many riders change the oil in the spring, when they're putting the bike back on the road, but really it should be changed just before the bike is laid up, so that the bearings are sitting in fresh oil. The same goes for the gearbox. If your airhead has a kickstart (a few did) turn the engine over slowly on the lever once a week, ignition off. Don't start it though – running the engine for a short time does more harm than good, as it produces a lot of moisture internally, which the engine doesn't get hot enough to burn off. That will attack the engine internals and the silencer.

Battery/electrics
Either remove the battery and give it a top-up charge every couple of weeks, or connect it up to a battery top-up device, such as the Optimate, which will keep it permanently fully charged. Damp conditions will allow fuses and earth connections to corrode, storing up electrical troubles for the spring. Eventually, wiring insulation will harden and fail.

Corrosion will take hold.

Brake caliper pistons will stick unless exercised now and then.

16 The Community

– key people, organisations and companies in the Boxer Twin world

Auctioneers

Bonhams www.bonhams.com
Cheffins www.cheffins.co.uk
eBay www.ebay.com
H&H www.classic-auctions.co.uk/www.classic-auctions.co.uk
Silver www.silverauctions.com

Clubs across the world

The BMW Club – UK & Ireland
www.thebmwclub.org.uk

BMW Motorcycle Owners of America
www.bmwmoa.org

BMW MC Berlin-Spandau – Germany
www.bmwmcs.de

BMW Clubs Australia
www.clubs.bmw.com.au

Beemers Motorcycle Club Hellas – Greece
www.beemers.gr

BMW Klubben Norge – Norway
www.bmwmc.no

BMW Moto Club – France
www.bmwmcf.com

BMW Motoclube – Portugal
www.bmwmotoclube.com

BMW Motorcycle Club of Iceland
www.bmwhjol.is

BMW Motorcycling Club of Finland
www.bmwmootoripyorakerho.fi

BMW Motorcycle Club – Singapore
www.bmwmcs.org

BMW Riders – Italy
www.bmwri.org

Club de Motos BMW de Espana – Spain
www.clubdemotosbmw.com

Svenska BMW MC Klubben – Sweden
www.bmw-mc-klubben.se

BMW Club Nederland – The Netherlands
www.clubnederland.nl

Specialists

We have restricted our listing to UK companies. This list does not imply recommendation and is not deemed to be comprehensive.

The Boxer Man – Leicester
www.boxerman.co.uk

Moto-Bins – Lincolnshire
www.motobins.co.uk

James Sherlock – Devon
www.james-sherlock.co.uk

Motorworks – Yorkshire
www.motorworks.co.uk

BM Bikes – website with lots of information
www.bmbikes.co.uk

Books

NB: Some of these books are out of print, but secondhand examples are available online.

BMW Twins – The Complete Story, Mick Walker, Crowood 1998

BMW Motorcycle Buyers Guide, Mark Zimmerman and Brian J. Nelson, Motorbooks 2003

Illustrated BMW Motorcycle Buyers Guide, Stefan Knittel and Roland Slabon, Motorbooks 1996

The BMW Boxer Twins 1970-1996 Bible, Ian Falloon, Veloce Publishing 2009

17 Vital statistics
– essential data at your fingertips

Listing the vital statistics of every BMW airhead variant would take more room than we have here, so we've picked three representative models: 1974 R75/6, 1980 R100RS and 1988 R65 Monolever.

Max speed
1974 R75/6: 107mph
1980 R100RS: 122mph
1988 R65 Monolever: 112mph (calculated)

Engine
1974 R75/6: air-cooled ohv flat-twin – 745cc. Bore and stroke 82 x 70.6mm. Compression ratio 9.0:1. Power 50bhp @ 6500rpm
1980 R100RS: air-cooled ohv flat-twin – 980cc. Bore and stroke 94 x 70.6mm. Compression ratio 8.2:1. Power 70bhp @ 7250rpm
1988 R65 Monolever: air-cooled ohv flat-twin – 650cc. Bore and stroke 82 x 61.5 mm. Compression ratio 8.7:1. Power 48bhp @ 7250rpm

Gearbox
1974 R75/6: five-speed, shaft drive
1980 R100RS: five-speed, shaft drive
1988 R65 Monolever: five-speed, shaft drive

Brakes
1974 R75/6: front 200mm disc, rear 200mm drum
1980 R100RS: front 260mm twin discs, rear 260mm disc
1988 R65 Monolever: front 285mm disc, rear 200mm drum

Electrics
1974 R75/6: 12-volt, alternator, cb points
1980 R100RS: 12-volt, alternator, cb points
1988 R65 Monolever: 12-volt, alternator, electronic ignition

Weight
1974 R75/6: 200kg
1980 R100RS: 210kg
1988 R65 Monolever: 209kg

Timeline
1969: R50/5, R60/5, R75/5 launched
1973: Wheelbase lengthened by 50mm
1974: R60/6, R75/6, R90/6, R90S launched
1975: Drilled brake discs, beefed up front forks, Hella switchgear, Magura dogleg levers
1977: R60/7, R75/7, R100/7, R100RS, R100S launched
1978: R100RT launched, R100T launched, R75/7 replaced by R80/7, twin front

discs on R100/7, rear disc and alloy wheels on R100RS
1979: R45, R65 launched
1981: Nikasil-coated bores, redesigned clutch, electronic ignition, Brembo disc
brakes replace ATE, R100CS launched
1982: R80RT, R65LS launched
1984: R65 and R80 and RT Monolever launched, R100s dropped
1986: R100RS reintroduced (60bhp)
1987: R100RT reintroduced (60bhp)
1991: R100R launched
1993: R80R launched
1994: R100R Mystic launched

Frame numbers

Model	Model year	Numbers
R50/5	1970/71	2900001-2903623
R50/5	1972/73	2903624-2910000
R60/5	1970/71	2930001-2938704
R60/5	1972/73	2938705-2950000
R75/5	1970/71	2970001-2982737
R75/5	1972/73	2982738-3000000
R75/5	1972/73	4000001-4010000
R60/6	1974	2910001-2920000
R60/6	1975	2920001-2930000
R60/6	1976	2960001-2970000
R60/6 (USA)	1974	4900001-4910000
R60/6 (USA)	1975	4920001-4925000
R60/6 (USA)	1976	4925001-4930000
R75/6	1974	4010001-4020000
R75/6	1975	4020001-4030000
R75/6	1976	4030001-4040000
R75/6 (USA)	1974	4910001-4920000
R75/6 (USA)	1975	4940001-4945000
R75/6 (USA)	1976	4945001-4950000
R90/6	1974	4040001-4050000
R90/6	1975	4050001-4060000
R90/6	1976	4060001-4070000
R90/6 (USA)	1974	4930001-4940000
R90/6 (USA)	1975	4960001-4970000
R90/6 (USA)	1976	4970001-4980000
R90S	1974	4070001-4080000
R90S	1975	4080001-4090000
R90S	1976	4090001-4100000
R90S (USA)	1974	4950001-4960000
R90S (USA)	1975	4980001-4990000
R90S (USA)	1976	4990001-5000000
R60/7	1977	6000001-6007000

Model	Model year	Numbers
R60/7	1978	6007001-6020000
R60/7	1979	6015001-6016000
R60/7 (USA)	1977	6100001-6101000
R60/7 (USA)	1978	6100001-6102000
R75/7	1977	6020001-6025000
R75/7	1978	6220000-6222000
R75/7	1979	6222001-6223000
R75/7 (USA)	1977	6120001-6122500
R80/7	1978	6200001-6205000
R80/7	1979-80	6205001-6207000
R80/7	1981-84	6012001-6015000
R80/7 (USA)	1978	6122501-6125000
R80/7 (USA)	1979	6126001-6128000
R80RT	1983-84	6420001-6425000
R80RT (USA)	1983-84	6172001-6175000
also		6186101-6186300
R100/7	1977	6040001-6045000
R100/7	1978	6045001-6050000
R100/7	1979-80	6050001-6054000
R100/7	1981-84	6035001-6040000
also		6400001-6405000
R100/7 (USA)	1977	6140001-6145000
R100/7 (USA)	1978	6145001-6150000
R100/7 (USA)	1979-80	6170001-6172000
R100/7 (USA)	1981-84	6175001-6178000
also		6186001-6186100
R100T	1978	6110001-6112000
R100T	1979-80	6150001-6152000
R100T	1981-84	6193001-6195000
R100T (USA)	1979-80	6103001-6104000
R100S	1977	6060001-6065000
R100S	1978	6065001-6070000
R100S	1979	6070001-6073000
R100S (USA)	1977	6160001-6162500
R100S (USA)	1978	6162501-6165000
R100S (USA)	1979-80	6165001-6167000
R100CS	1981-84	6135001-6140000
R100CS (USA)	1981-84	6188001-6190000
R100RS	1977	6080001-6082000
R100RS	1978	6082501-6086000
also		6086001-6095000
R100RS	1979-80	6095001-6100000
also		6223001-6224000
R100RS	1981-84	6075001-6080000
also		6390001-6397000

Model	Model year	Numbers
R100RS (USA)	1977	6180001-6182500
R100RS (USA)	1978	6182501-6185000
R100RS (USA)	1979-80	6185001-6186000
R100RS (USA)	1981-84	6225001-6229000
also		6308001-6308100
R100RT	1978	6115001-6117000
R100RT	1979-80	6152001-6153000
also		6152001-6160000
also		6168001-6170000
R100RT	1981-84	6230001-6240000
R100RT (USA)	1978	6190001-6193000
R100RT (USA)	1979-80	6195001-6199000
R100RT (USA)	1981-84	6240001-6245000
R45	1979-80	6300001-6308000
R45	1981-85	6270001-6276000
R65	1978-80	6340001-6350000
R65	1981-85	6310001-6320000
also		6410001-6415000
R65 (USA)	1979-80	6380001-6385000
R65 (USA)	1981-85	6385001-6390000
also		6399950-6400000
R65LS	1982-85	6350001-6355000
R65LS (USA)	1982-85	6370001-6372000
Monolever	**1984/5 on**	
R65RT	1986 on	6460001-6461500
R80	1985 on	6440001-6449000
R80RT	1985 on	6470001-6480000
also		6483001-6486000
R80 (USA)	1985 on	6480001-6483000
R80RT (USA)	1985 on	6490001-6493000
R100RS	1987 on	0160001-0163000
R100RT	1988 on	6016001-6018000
R100RS (USA)	1988 on	6247001-6248000
R100RT (USA)	1988 on	6292601-6294000

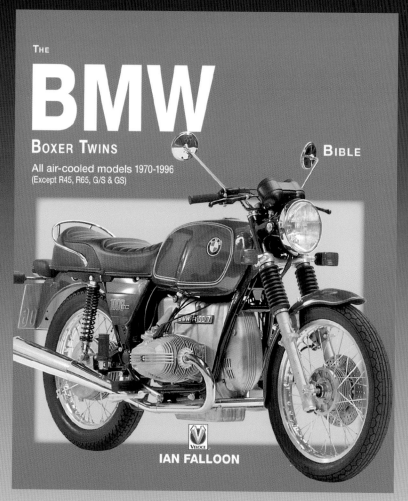

The

BMW

BOXER TWINS   BIBLE

All air-cooled models 1970-1996
(Except R45, R65, G/S & GS)

IAN FALLOON

ISBN: 978-1-845849-99-3
Paperback • 25x20.7cm • 160 pages • 190 colour and b&w pictures

The air-cooled boxer BMW twins were among the most significant motorcycles of the 1970s through the 1980s, providing an unparalleled combination of comfort, reliability, and performance. From the /5 series, a complete series of sport and touring motorcycles evolved that earned a huge following and which was never emulated by other manufacturers.

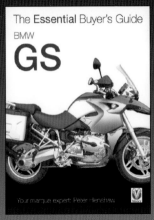

The Essential Buyer's Guide

BMW
GS

Your marque expert: Peter Henshaw

ISBN: 978-1-84584-135-5

The Essential Buyer's Guide

BSA
500 & 650 Twins
A7, A10, A50 & A65: 1946 to 1973

Your marque expert: Peter Henshaw

ISBN: 978-1-84584-136-2

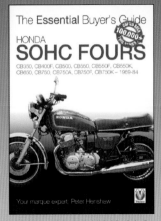

The Essential Buyer's Guide

HONDA
SOHC FOURS
CB350, CB400F, CB500, CB550, CB550F, CB550K,
CB650, CB750, CB750A, CB750F, CB750K – 1969-84

Your marque expert: Peter Henshaw

ISBN: 978-1-845842-84-0

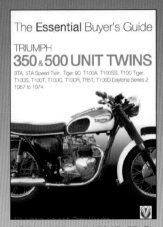

The Essential Buyer's Guide

TRIUMPH
350 & 500 UNIT TWINS
3TA, 5TA Speed Twin, Tiger 90, T100A, T100SS, T100 Tiger,
T100S, T100T, T100C, T100R, TR5T, T100D Daytona Series 2
1957 to 1974

Your marque expert: Peter Henshaw

ISBN: 978-1-845847-55-5

Having these books in your pocket is like having a real marque expert by your side. Benefit from the authors' years of real ownership experience, learn how to spot a bad motorcycle or scooter quickly, and how to assess a promising one like a professional.
Get the right bike at the right price!

For more information and price details see our website: www.veloce.co.uk

Index